# Nature Near and Far

HOUGHTON MIFFLIN HARCOURT
School Publishers

# Contents

# Seth and Beth

by Anna Guzman

illustrated by Piero Corva

Seth and Beth met at the path.
Beth has a big map. It can help.
They will go and see Bob Frog.

This trip is far.
Seth and Beth pass Ben.  Ben
can see them.  Seth tips his cap.
Then Ben tips his cap.

This trip is far.

Beth and Seth pass Sam. Sam
can see them. Seth and Sam tip
their hats.

Beth and Seth pass Huck Duck.
They are at Blue Pond. Huck
can see them.
"Where is Bob Frog?" Beth yells.

"Does Bob Frog live here?"
Seth asks.
"Bob Frog is in this pond,"
Huck quacks.

"Get up, Bob Frog!" Seth and
Beth call. "Play with us! This is
fun! It is fun."

# Zeb Yak

by Jane Tyler
illustrated by Katherine Lucas

This is Zeb. Zeb is a yak. Zeb is
a little yak. Zeb is not big yet.

Zeb will get big and look like this.
Zeb will be like his big dad.  Then
Zeb will go thud, thud, thud.

Zeb is with his mom. His mom will eat grass. Zeb can eat grass. Then Zeb and Mom will nap.

Zeb and his mom and dad live
on this cold hill.  Lots of yaks live
with Zeb and his mom and dad.
Yaks cut big paths on the hill.

Big yaks go thump, thump, thump.
Big yaks go thud, thud, thud.
The paths get big.  No grass is on
this yak path.

Zeb can look up.  Zeb can see
lots of blue.  Zeb can see the sun.
Zeb is one glad yak!  Zeb will go
thud, thud, thud.

# The Duck Nest

by Michael Frost
illustrated by Joe Cepeda

Beth Ann was with Gram.
Beth Ann jumped and jumped.
Then Beth Ann quit jumping!

"Is that a nest?" Beth Ann
asked Gram.

"Yes," said Gram. "It is a
duck nest filled with eggs."

"Gram, is that egg cracked?"
asked Beth Ann.
"Yes," said Gram. "That egg
has lots of cracks."

"Look at this little duck!"
said Gram.
"Where is its mom?" Beth Ann
asked. "I bet it misses its mom."

"Not far," said Gram. "That big duck must be its mom. She will not come back with us here." Gram and Beth Ann left.

Mom Duck had a bug.
Did that little duck get that bug?
Yes!  Yum!  Yum!

# Animal Moms

by James Wang

This mom has pups. She is
resting on the rocks with them.
Rest, pups. Rest, mom.

This mom has cubs. The cubs
are just like their mom. They can
swim in this cold water! Swim,
cubs. Swim, mom.

This mom is hunting with her cubs.
What is jumping in that water?
Hunt, cubs! Grab a snack!

This mom is with her kits. They
swim in a pond. Their pond has
lots of sticks, grasses, and twigs.
Swim, kits. Swim, mom.

This mom is with her pups.
Their pond is filled with mud.
They can swim fast in wet mud.
Swim, pups.  Swim, mom.

This mom is with her little ducks.
Ducks swim and swim. It is fun.
Have fun, ducks! Swim, swim, swim!

26

# Scratch, Chomp

by Edward Bonfanti

illustrated by Rick Brown

Chuck and his dad went off on a
trip.  At Finch Pond, Chuck and
his dad played catch.  Chuck has
a fast pitch.

Dad can catch, but Dad did not
catch this pitch.
"You never miss, Dad. Why did
you miss?" Chuck asks.

"I hear scratch, scratch, chomp,
chomp.  Do you?" asks Dad.
"Yes!  Scratch, scratch, chomp,
chomp.  What is it?" asks Chuck.

Scratch, scratch, scratch. Chomp, chomp, chomp. Can Chuck and Dad find out what is scratching and chomping?

30

Scratch, scratch, chomp, chomp.
Chuck and Dad can see a stump
and lots of chips.  A big brown
lump is in the pond.

The lump has an animal on it.
This animal can scratch, scratch,
scratch.  It can chop, chop, chop,
chop.  It can chomp, chomp,
chomp.  Can you tell what it is?

# Rich Gets a Dog

by Rick Eduardo

illustrated by Beth Spiegel

Mom and Dad tucked Rich in bed.

"Can I get a dog?" asked Rich.

"Hmmm," said Dad.

"Hmmm," said Mom.

Then Mom and Dad said yes.
Rich sat up in bed.  Mom, Dad,
and Rich like dogs very much.

Today, Mom and Dad will get Rich
a dog.  Rich can see dogs, dogs,
dogs.  Rich can get just one dog.

Here are big dogs and small
dogs.  Here are fat dogs and
thin dogs.  Dogs, dogs, dogs!

Rich picks a brown dog called
Fletch. Fletch is big and can
run fast. Rich has his own dog!

Rich hugs Fletch. Fletch and Rich
will be pals.

# Champs

by John Cross
illustrated by Randy Cecil

Dutch is Bill's dog.
Dutch and Bill play tug.
Dutch is the tug champ.

Bill sits on his bench to rest.
Dutch has his own spot to rest.
Dutch's spot is not a bench.

Fran is here. Fran is Bill's pal.
Chet is Fran's dog. Dutch and
Chet play. Bill and Fran chat.

Dutch and Chet like to play with
Bill and Fran.  Dutch and Chet
get set to play catch.  They know
Bill and Fran will play with them.

"Catch it, Dutch!" yells Bill.
Dutch jumps up, up, up to catch.
Then Fran yells, "Catch it, Chet!"
Chet jumps and catches, too.

It has been such fun!  Chet
and Dutch are such good
dogs!  They are champs!

# Kits, Chicks, and Pups

by Lara Heisman

Cats, dogs, and ducks have
moms and dads.

Dog moms have pups. This mom
and her pups sit still. They make
such a good picture.

Ducks do not have pups.  Ducks
have chicks.  Ducks swim in a
pond.  Dad duck is with his chicks.

This mom duck has a nest. Eggs will hatch in it. Chicks will pop out! Mom will get off the nest.

This kit can run. Mom cat will
run, too. The kit and her mom
will run and then stop and nap.

This mom and dad know that
chicks must eat.  This mom's chicks
will get fed.  Mom and dad will
do it.  The chicks will get big.

# Phil's New Bat

by Edward Bonfanti

illustrated by Jennifer H. Hayden

Phil's dad got him a new bat.
It was just what Phil wished for!

When Phil got his new bat, he
hit with it.  When Phil got a hit,
his bat went, "Wham!  Bash!"

Phil got many hits and runs. His
mom and his dad and his pal had
fun! Did Phil get a hit? Yes!

Did Phil fall?  Yes!  Phil fell
down on his leg.  Phil cannot
play with his bat for a bit.

Phil is not sad.  If Phil cannot
play with his bat, Phil will let his
pal play with it.

Phil's bat is in good hands.
Phil and his dad can play catch.
You do not catch with a bat!

# In a Rush

by Sue De Marco

illustrated by Maria Maddocks

Shan is in a rush. She has to splash in cold, wet slush. She goes splish, splash, splish, splash.

Wham! Slip! Slop! Bash! Shan
fell down in the wet slush. Shan
just sat in slush. It felt like mush.

Then Shan got up. Shan did not
rush. Shan did not dash in the
wet slush. Shan went plop, plod.

Plop, plop, plod. Shan must get to Phil's Best Stuff Shop. That shop has lots and lots of stuff. Shan must get to that shop.

Phil's Best Stuff Shop is still open!
Shan got to it at last. Shan will
rush in. Shan has cash. What
new stuff will Shan get?

Look at Shan! Shan is all in
yellow. Slush is fun now. Shan
is glad. Splish, splash, splish,
splash, Shan!

# Ralph Goes to Camp

by Adam Feldman
illustrated by Barry Gott

Ralph asks his mom and
dad if he can go to camp.
"Yes," said Dad, "if you
do some jobs."

Ralph was shocked.

"Jobs?" Ralph asked.

"Yes," said Dad, "but it isn't
that bad. It's just the dog and
the trash."

Shep is Ralph's dog. Ralph had to
give Shep a bath. Shep had fun
splishing and splashing. Ralph got
wet, but Ralph did his job well.

When Ralph had to tug big
trash bins, he didn't rush. Ralph
didn't spill trash. Ralph didn't
trip. Ralph did his job well.

"Ralph goes to camp today!"
said Ralph's mom.
Ralph got his yellow bag and hat.

Ralph went to camp at
last! Ralph had fun at
camp, and he had no jobs!

# Trish's Gift

by Bryn Haddock

illustrated by Mircea Catusanu

When Trish was ten, Gramps sent
a gift. Trish and Mom opened it.
It was a new desk.

"Dad," said Trish, "Gramps sent
this desk with brass trim, but I
can't sit at it."
"Let's see that desk with brass
trim," said Dad.

"Back when I was just ten," said
Dad, "I had a bench with brass
trim on it. I got big, but that
bench with brass trim didn't
grow big."
"Where is that bench?" asked Trish.

"Gramps put that bench in his shed," said Dad.

"Is that the shed Gramps had?" asked Trish.

"Yes, it's his shed," said Dad.

Dad and Trish ran fast.

Trish and Dad hunted and hunted.
Then Dad lifted up a big green
cloth.
"That's it!" yelled Trish.

"Did Gramps know that we
had this bench with brass trim?"
asked Trish.

"We can ask him," said Dad.

"Let's call Gramps and ask."

# Tate's Cakes

by Bruce Falcon
illustrated by Peter Grosshauser

Tate had never made a cake.
Tate did know that cakes must
bake. Can Tate make cakes?

"This sand is hot, hot, hot. Cakes
can bake in it. What goes into
cakes? If Wade has made cakes,
Wade will tell me," said Tate.

"Well, I never made a cake,"
said Wade. "Let's ask Jade. If
Jade has made cakes, Jade will
tell us."

"Yes," said Tate, "let's ask Jade."

Wade and Tate went to Jade's big cave. Jade was in.

"I am glad you came," said Jade.

"I just made ten cakes."

"This cake is on sale. That cake is
on sale and that cake is on sale.
The big cakes are all on sale,"
Jade said. "I just made them."

Wade got four cakes. Tate got five cakes. Jade's bake sale was over. Tate and Wade ate Jade's cakes. Tate and Wade never did make cakes. They ate Jade's.

# Dave and the Whales

by Andrew Hathaway
illustrated by Julia Woolf

Dave is a whale. Dave is fast.
"Let's play," Dave yelled. "Chase
me! Chase, chase, chase me!"

Dave's pals watch.  Not one whale
is as fast as Dave is.  Dave did
not get his pals to chase him.
"Why chase Dave?" asked Jake.
"We can't catch him."

Dave made waves as big as hills.
"Let's make waves!" yelled Dave.
"Why?" asked Lane.  "We can't
make waves as big as Dave's."
Dave did not get his pals to make
waves.

Dave is sad. His pals will not play with him.

"I get it," said Dave. "I am fast and can make big waves. But, I can't sing!"

"Let's sing!" yelled Dave.
Two whales came.  Three whales
came.  Then four and five whales
came.

"Sing, whales!" yelled Dave. "Let's make a tape. Let's name it Dave and the Whales! It will be a big hit!"

# A Safe Lodge

by Elizabeth Pearson

This is an animal that can make its own lodge.  It starts with sticks.

This animal cuts sticks.  It
drags the sticks and makes a
big lodge with them.

This lodge is a safe place.
It is in a lake. It is made
of sticks and mud.

This lodge has space for kits. Kits romp and rest. When kits get big, they can go out. They can watch Dad and Mom cut sticks.

Big kits can cut sticks. Kits can drag sticks and help make a dam. A dam holds water back.

Mom, Dad, and the kits made this dam. If water spills over it, Mom, Dad, and the kits will fix it. This dam helps make their lodge safe.

# The Race

by Carre Murray
illustrated by Jerry Smath

This race is fun to watch. Get
into the fun! Yell, yell. Clap,
clap. Race, race, race!

Dave and Ace got in this race.
Dave will run fast. Ace will run
fast. Crack! The race starts.
Dave and Ace take off.

Dave has a lane. It is his space.
Ace has a lane. It is his space.
They must run and jump in that
lane. They can't trade lanes.

Madge and Grace got in this
race. They will skate fast. Go,
Madge! Go, Grace! Skate as
fast as you can. Race, race, race.

96

Blake and Trace got in this race.

Blake and Trace set the pace.

Will Trace race past Blake?  Go,

Blake!  Go, Trace!

The last race is over. Madge, Grace, Blake, Trace, Dave, and Ace sit in the shade. The judge gave two of them red badges and four of them blue badges.

# Mike's Bike

by Claire Coolidge
illustrated by Jill Dubin

Mike's new bike is red and white.
Mike just got it. Mike can ride
it well. Mike rides his bike
with pride.

Mike will ride his bike to see Nell.
His dad will ride with him. Nell
will like Mike's bike. Nell's bike is
red and white, too.

Nell did like Mike's bike.
"I like its white stripes. Mine
has red stripes. Both bikes have
stripes," Nell said.

Mike, Dad, and Nell take a ride.
"This bike path is fun. I like it,"
said Mike. "It is nice to ride on."
"I like it too," said Nell.

Dad, Nell, and Mike ride for five
or six miles. It is a long ride.
"This is the end," said Nell. "It is
time to go back."

They stop at Nell's place.

"That was fun, Mike," said Nell.

Mike had a big, wide grin on
his face.

"Best time of my life!" said Mike.

# The Nest

by Amy Long

This big bird has a name. His name is Pale Male. Pale Male's chest is white. Pale Male's neck is white.

Pale Male has a nest. The nest is wide. It is a big, big nest. Pale Male made it. It can take a long time to make a big nest like this.

If you walk past it, look up. Pale Male's nest is not just a big pile of sticks and vines. It is a fine nest.

The nest had eggs in it. It has small chicks in it now. Dad and Mom find mice for them. Those chicks get quite big, as big as Mom and Dad.

It is time to fly. Chicks grasp the
nest at its side. Chicks flap and
flap and flap. Then they let go
and glide. Glide, flap, flap, glide.
Both can fly!

This big chick can fly like Mom and Dad. This chick can rise up and dip down. Rise and dive, chick. Rise and glide, chick. Fly!

# The Nice Vet

by Vince Delacroix
illustrated by Dave Klug

Kate's dog Spike has an itch.
Spike rubs and rubs his eyes.
Kate calls Spike's vet.

"Spike has an itch," Kate tells Spike's vet. "Spike rubs and rubs his eyes." The vet has time to see Spike.

Kate and Spike walk fast.
Kate's mom goes with them.
Spike still has an itch.
Spike whines and whines.

At last, they get to the vet's
place. It's not a long walk.
"I can fix Spike's itch," the vet tells
Kate. "I will make his eyes numb."

Spike's vet puts five drops
in Spike's eyes.  Spike's
eyes stop itching!  The vet
writes in Spike's file.

Kate hands Spike's vet a dime.
Nice price, isn't it? Who is Spike's
nice vet? It's Kate's dad!

# Kite Time

by Zach Mathews

illustrated by Chi Chung

The wind is up. It's time to fly a
kite. It's kite time! It's fun time!

A kite can ride on the wind.  It can glide up on the wind.  Wind takes a kite up and up.  Wind can knock it down, too.

118

A kite can dip down. Then it can
rise back up. A kite can dip or
rise. It can rise, dip, and rise.
Wind can play with it.

119

Make fists and run with the kite's line in them. Run with it. Run, run, run. Run fast! Then the kite will fly like a bird. Up, up, up it will rise.

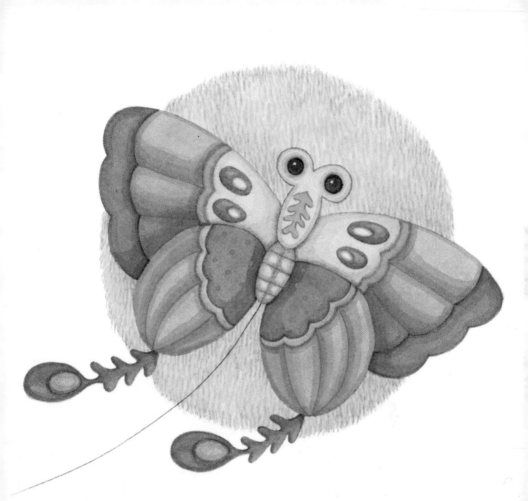

It is up. Then it dips. It is up.
Then it glides. It is up. Then it
dives. It is up. Then it slides.
Hold on to the kite's line. Do not
let it go!

If the wind stops, it's time to quit.
Wrap up the kites.

# Word Lists

## Seth and Beth
page 3

**Decodable Words**
Target Skill: Digraph *th*
Beth, path, Seth, them, then, this, with

**Previously Taught Skills**
and, asks, at, Ben, big, Bob, can, cap, Duck, Frog, fun, get, has, hats, help, his, Huck, in, is, it, map, met, pass, pond, quacks, Sam, tip, tips, trip, up, us, will, yells

**High-Frequency Words**
New
blue, far, live, their, where

Previously Taught
a, are, call, does, go, here, play, see, the, they

## Zeb Yak
page 9

**Decodable Words**
Target Skill: Digraph *th*
path, paths, then, this, thud, thump, with

**Previously Taught Skills**
and, big, can, cut, dad, get, glad, grass, hill, his, is, lots, mom, nap, not, on, sun, up, will, yak, yaks, yet, Zeb

**High-Frequency Words**
New
blue, cold, little, live

Previously Taught
a, be, eat, go, like, look, no, of, one, see, the

Accompanies *"Sea Animals"*

# The Duck Nest

page 15

### Decodable Words
Target Skill: Endings *-s, -es, -ed, -ing*
asked, cracked, cracks, eggs, filled, its, jumped, jumping, lots, misses

Target Skill: Digraph *th*
Beth, that, then, this, with

### Previously Taught Skills
and, Ann, at, back, bet, big, bug, did, duck, egg, get, Gram, has, had, is, it, left, lots, mom, must, nest, not, quit, us, will, yes, yum

### High-Frequency Words
New
far, little, where

Previously Taught
a, be, come, here, I, look, of, said, she, was

# Animal Moms

page 21

### Decodable Words
Target Skill: Endings *-s, -es, -ed, -ing*
cubs, ducks, filled, grasses, hunting, jumping, kits, lots, pups, resting, rocks, sticks, twigs

Target Skill: Digraph *th*
that, them, this, with

### Previously Taught Skills
and, can, fast, fun, grab, has, hunt, in, is, it, just, mom, mud, on, pond, rest, snack, swim, wet

### High-Frequency Words
New
cold, little, their, water

Previously Taught
a, are, have, her, like, of, she, the, they, what

## Scratch, Chomp

page 27

### Decodable Words
Target Skills: Digraphs *ch*, *tch*
catch, chips, chomp, chomping, chop, Chuck, Finch, pitch, scratch, scratching

### Previously Taught Skills
an, and, asks, at, big, but, can, dad, did, fast, has, his, in, is, it, lots, lump, miss, not, off, on, pond, stump, tell, this, trip, went, yes

### High-Frequency Words
New
brown, never, off, out

Previously Taught
a, animal, do, find, hear, I, of, played, see, the, what, why, you

## Rich Gets a Dog

page 33

### Decodable Words
Target Skills: Digraphs *ch*, *tch*
Fletch, much, Rich

### Previously Taught Skills
and, asked, bed, big, can, Dad, dog, dogs, fast, fat, get, has, his, Hmmm, hugs, in, is, just, Mom, pals, picks run, sat, then, thin, tucked, up, will, yes

### High-Frequency Words
New
brown, own, very

Previously Taught
a, are, be, called, here, I, like, one, said, see, small, today

# Champs

page 39

**Decodable Words**
Target Skill: Possessives with 's
Bill's, Dutch's, Fran's

Target Skills: Digraphs *ch*, *tch*
bench, catch, catches, champ, champs, chat, Chet, Dutch, such

Previously Taught Skills
and, Bill, dog, dogs, Fran, fun, get, has, his, is, it, jumps, not, on, pal, rest, set, sits, spot, them, then, tug, up, will, with, yells

**High-Frequency Words**
New
been, know, own

Previously Taught
a, are, good, here, like, play, the, they, to, too

# Kits, Chicks, and Pups

page 45

**Decodable Words**
Target Skill: Possessives with 's
mom's

Target Skills: Digraphs *ch*, *tch*
chicks, hatch, such

Previously Taught Skills
and, big, can, cat, cats, dad, dads, dog, dogs, duck, ducks, eggs, fed, get, has, his, in, is, it, kit, mom, moms, must, nap, nest, not, off, pond, pop, pups, run, sit, still, stop, swim, that, then, this, will, with

**High-Frequency Words**
New
know, off, out

Previously Taught
a, do, eat, good, have, her, make, picture, the, they, too

## Phil's New Bat
page 51

**Decodable Words**
Target Skills: Digraphs *sh*, *wh*, *ph*
bash, Phil, Phil's, wham, when, wished

Previously Taught Skills
and, bat, bit, can, cannot, catch, dad,
did, fell, fun, get, got, had, hands, him,
his, hit, hits, if, in, is, it, just, leg, let,
mom, not, on, pal, runs, sad, went, will,
with, yes

**High-Frequency Words**
New
down, fall, new

Previously Taught
a, do, for, good, he, many,
play, was, what, you

## In a Rush
page 57

**Decodable Words**
Target Skills: Digraphs *sh*, *wh*, *ph*
bash, cash, dash, mush, Phil's, rush,
Shan, shop, slush, splash, splish, wham

Previously Taught Skills
and, at, best, did, fell, felt, fun, get, glad,
got, has, in, is, it, just, last, lots, must,
not, plod, plop, sat, slip, slop, still, stuff,
that, then, up, went, wet, will

**High-Frequency Words**
New
down, goes, new, open,
yellow

Previously Taught
a, all, cold, like, look, now,
of, she, the, to, what

# Ralph Goes to Camp

page 63

### Decodable Words
**Target Skill: Contractions** *'s, n't*
didn't, isn't, it's

**Target Skills: Digraphs** *sh, wh, ph*
Ralph, Ralph's, rush, Shep, shocked,
splashing, splishing, trash, when

**Previously Taught Skills**
and, asked, asks, at, bad, bag, bath, big,
bins, but, camp, can, dad, did, dog, fun,
got, had, hat, his, if, is, it, job, jobs, just,
last, mom, spill, that, trip, tub, well,
went, wet, yes

### High-Frequency Words
**New**
goes, yellow

**Previously Taught**
do, give, go, he, no, said,
some, the, to, today, was,
you

# Trish's Gift

page 69

### Decodable Words
**Target Skill: Contractions** *'s, n't*
can't, didn't, it's, let's, that's

**Target Skills: Digraphs** *sh, wh*
shed, Trish, when

**Previously Taught Skills**
and, ask, asked, at, back, bench, big,
brass, but, can, cloth, Dad, desk, did,
fast, gift, got, Gramps, had, him, his,
hunted, in, is, it, just, lifted, Mom, on,
ran, sent, sit, ten, that, then, this, trim,
up, with, yelled, yes

### High-Frequency Words
**New**
green, grow, new, opened

**Previously Taught**
a, call, I, know, put, said,
see, the, was, we, where

128

# Tate's Cakes

page 75

## Decodable Words
**Target Skill:** Long *a* (CVC*e*)
ate, bake, cake, cakes, came, cave, Jade, Jade's, made, make, sale, Tate, Wade

## Previously Taught Skills
am, and, ask, big, can, did, glad, got, had, has, hot, if, in, is, it, just, let's, must, on, sand, tell, ten, that, them, this, us, well, went, will, yes

## High-Frequency Words
**New**
five, four, into, over

**Previously Taught**
a, all, are, goes, I, know, me, never, said, the, they, to, was, what, you

# Dave and the Whales

page 81

## Decodable Words
**Target Skill:** Long *a* (CVC*e*)
came, chase, Dave, Dave's, Jake, Lane, made, make, name, tape, waves, whale, whales

## Previously Taught Skills
am, and, as, asked, big, but, can, can't, catch, did, fast, get, hills, him, his, hit, is, it, let's, not, pals, sad, then, will, with, yelled

## High-Frequency Words
**New**
five, four, three, two, watch

**Previously Taught**
a, be, I, me, one, play, said, sing, the, to, we, why

# A Safe Lodge

page 87

## Decodable Words
Target Skills: Soft *c*, *g*, *dge*
lodge, place, space

Target Skill: Long *a* (CVC*e*)
lake, made, make, makes, place, safe, space

Previously Taught Skills
an, and, back, big, can, cut, cuts, Dad, dam, drag, drags, fix, get, has, help, helps, if, in, is, it, its, kits, Mom, mud, rest, romp, spills, sticks, that, them, this, when, will, with

## High-Frequency Words
New
over, starts, watch

Previously Taught
a, animal, for, go, holds, of, out, own, the, their, they, water

# The Race

page 93

## Decodable Words
Target Skills: Soft *c*, *g*, *dge*
Ace, badges, Grace, judge, Madge, pace, race, space, Trace

Target Skill: Long *a* (CVC*e*)
Ace, Blake, Dave, gave, Grace, lane, lanes, pace, race, shade, skate, space, take, Trace, trade

Previously Taught Skills
and, as, can, can't, clap, crack, fast, fun, get, got, has, his, in, is, it, jump, last, must, past, red, run, set, sit, that, them, this, will, yell

## High-Frequency Words
New
four, into, over, starts, two, watch

Previously Taught
a, blue, go, of, off, the, they, to, you

## Mike's Bike

page 99

### Decodable Words
Target Skill: Long *i* (CVC*e*)
bike, bikes, five, life, like, Mike, Mike's, miles, mine, nice, pride, ride, rides, stripes, time, white, wide

### Previously Taught Skills
and, at, back, best, big, can, dad, did, end, face, fun, got, grin, had, has, him, his, is, it, its, just, Nell, Nell's, on, path, place, red, six, stop, take, that, this, well, will, with

### High-Frequency Words
New
both, long, or

Previously Taught
a, for, go, have, I, my, new, of, said, see, the, they, to, too, was

## The Nest

page 105

### Decodable Words
Target Skill: Long *i* (CVC*e*)
dive, fine, glide, like, mice, pile, quite, rise, side, time, vines, white, wide

### Previously Taught Skills
and, as, at, big, can, chest, chick, chicks, Dad, dip, eggs, flap, get, grasp, had, has, his, if, in, is, it, its, just, let, make, made, Male, Male's, Mom, name, neck, nest, not, Pale, past, sticks, take, them, then, this, up

### High-Frequency Words
New
bird, both, fly, long, those, walk

Previously Taught
a, down, find, for, go, look, now, of, small, the, they, to, you

# The Nice Vet

page 111

## Decodable Words
Target Skill: Digraphs *mb, wr*
numb, writes

Target Skill: Long *i* (CVC*e*)
dime, file, five, nice, price, Spike,
Spike's, time, whines, writes

### Previously Taught Skills
an, and, at, can, dad, dog, drops, fast,
fix, get, hands, has, his, in, is, isn't,
it, itch, itching, it's, Kate, Kate's, last,
make, mom, not, place, rubs, still,
stops, tells, them, vet, vet's, will, with

## High-Frequency Words
New
eyes, long, walk

Previously Taught
a, calls, goes, I, puts, see,
the, they, to, who

# Kite Time

page 117

## Decodable Words
Target Skill: Digraphs *kn, wr*
knock, wrap

Target Skill: Long *i* (CVC*e*)
dives, glide, glides, kite, kite's, kites,
like, line, ride, rise, slides, time

### Previously Taught Skills
and, back, can, dip, dips, fast, fists, fun,
if, in, is, it, it's, let, make, not, on, quit,
run, stops, takes, them, then, up, will,
wind, with

## High-Frequency Words
New
bird, fly, or

Previously Taught
a, do, down, go, hold, play,
the, to, too